Charles F Cutting

Glimpses of Scandinavia and Russia

Charles F Cutting

Glimpses of Scandinavia and Russia

ISBN/EAN: 9783337297145

Printed in Europe, USA, Canada, Australia, Japan

Cover: Foto ©ninafisch / pixelio.de

More available books at **www.hansebooks.com**

GLIMPSES OF

SCANDINAVIA AND RUSSIA

BY

CHAS F CUTTING

*En écrivant mes souvenirs, je me rapellerai le
temps passé, qui doublera, pour ainsi dire, mon
existence.*
J J ROUSSEAU

BOSTON

THOMAS GROOM & COMPANY PUBLISHERS

INDIA BUILDING 82 STATE STREET

1887

THE following pages are extracts from a journal written hastily, at odd moments, during a rapid journey in the summer of 1887. The majority of them were written in my stateroom, or while riding in a railway carriage, after a hard day's sight-seeing. The fragmentary character of the descriptions does such injustice to the places visited that I, even at the last moment, hesitate to commit them to print; but the kindly expressed wishes of my friends, and also the almost total absence of guide books of these countries, have prevailed upon me to hope that I might perhaps awaken a curiosity to visit these wondrous regions, and thus indirectly be the means of giving as rare a pleasure to others as the journey has afforded me.

C. F. C.

LONGWOOD, December 1st, 1887.

Scandinavia and Russia.

*T*HERE is nothing new to write in these days of the crossing of the Atlantic. In such magnificent ships as the *Umbria* and *Etruria* it is reduced to a matter of hours, and the passages are made with the regularity of ferry-boats.

We had an uneventful trip on the latter, with Capt. Cook ; leaving New York on a Saturday morning and lunching in Liverpool the following Saturday, at two P. M. At five, we left by train for Hull, where we arrived promptly at ten the same evening, and were thus in the Station Hotel in just seven days and nine hours from the time of leaving the Metropolitan Hotel in New York, having in the mean time crossed the Atlantic and the whole of England, with a delay of one hour at Queenstown and three hours in Liverpool.

The day is so very warm that I do not go out. V—— and B—— are in London, expecting to meet me here Wednesday next, to sail on the *Domino*, of the Wilson Line, for Norway and the North Cape. How I do long to get away! The hotel is stupid and hot, without a soul to be seen in its large, pleasant hall and waiting-rooms. The maids are all chatting together in the serving-room, on my floor, with nothing to do. The waiters in the coffee-room are asleep. It is one of those large, fine hotels, managed by the railroad companies, and adjoining the terminus, so common in England. It is very comfortable, very cheerless, very lonely. Have serious thoughts of hunting up the American Consul, if there is one in Hull, for the mere sake of something to do ; but the streets, as seen from the windows, appear equally deserted and uninteresting, and thoughts that necessitate exercise, however serious, vanish upon consulting the thermometer. A Sunday in a provincial, commercial town in England, without friends, is indeed a *holy* day !

I could endure it no longer in Hull, and after

making all my arrangements with the steamer people this morning, I left my heavy luggage behind, and came north by train, one and three-quarter hours, to

SCARBOROUGH.

How can I describe this unique and lovely spot! A broad, sandy beach, about the length of Newport's first beach, is enclosed by high cliffs, as at Dover; at the top and bottom of which are broad asphalt and macadamized promenades and drive-ways, connected at intervals by almost vertical tramways. In front is the broad expanse of the North Sea, covered with pleasure-boats of all descriptions. The cliffs are terraced with ornamental masonry, and laid out in groves and gardens, through which wind interminable, zigzag walks, quite to the very top, which tax the strength of the strongest man to ascend. A large part of one side is occupied by the Spa Garden, with terraced theatre and casino, kiosks, band stand, rustic bridges, and heavy sea-wall of sandstones. On the other side the foundations of the Grand Hotel are built, receding from the water, story on story, like one side of a huge pyramid, to the crest of the cliff, on top of which is the hotel building proper ; the top of each story forming delightful and lofty promenade balconies, which command the striking views òf this magnificent natural amphitheatre.

The North Cliff, which encloses the bay on one side, has along its crest, and extending down to the water's edge, a ruined, old, machicolated wall, which adds not a little to the general picturesqueness. At its foot the larger ships and craft lie gathered in safety, protected by a solid breakwater of masonry.

To the south, the cliffs extend one after another down the coast, until they are lost in the distance.

And now comes the finest feature of all. In the centre of the amphitheatre, and parting the cliffs to the very sands on the beach, is a broad gorge, or ravine, extending up and back through the town, and far inland. This is exquisitely laid out as a public valley park, with clustering, dense shade-trees, which afford delightful cool retreats amongst flowers and velvety lawn. This ravine is crossed by two lofty, airy, ornamental, iron viaducts, which connect the two parts of the town.

The residences are on the top of the cliffs, — fine, solid English houses, with only a driveway between them and the edge of the declivity.

As one sits on the terraces in the long twilight of these latitudes, listening to the music of the Spa Band, to the distant breaking of the water on the beach far below, to the answering call of the fisherman to a passing boat, or to the singing of happy pleasure-seekers floating idly over the waters of the bay in their gaily decked yachts; with the magnificent panorama of the broad, boundless sea and the terraced shore before one, — it is hard to realize that there is, anywhere, a world of toil and care and worry, and that these moments of great enjoyment are only a short but never-to-be-forgotten day-dream.

This afternoon, walked up through the narrow July 5. lanes of the old town to the church, and then on to the castle on the North Cliff. It is a picturesque and lofty ruin of an old Norman building; surrounded by walls; now used — what part of it is still habitable — as a military depot for stores. In what was the old castle-yard, a fine, large, green plot, on the very crest of the cliff as it stretches out into the sea, volunteers were encamped. Squads were being drilled; others were practising cannon-firing at a floating target far below on the water.

From this crest, the view north is quite as extensive as toward the south. Another beach, from the
middle of which juts out a long iron promenade pier,
with the houses on the shore, forms what is called
North Scarborough. It is not, however, a fashionable quarter, nor does it compare in beauty with the
situation of the main town.

I have been all over the shore, cliffs, and valley,
again and again, to-day, and can only still marvel at
the very striking features of the place, it combines
so many and varied attractions, the sights are all so
thoroughly characteristic. The old fishermen and
boys in the fish-market on the open beach ; the tiny
donkeys standing patiently in the sands for the children to amble about on, with horses alongside for
their elders ; bath-houses on wheels, dragged in and
out of the water by horses, while the occupants are
inside ; landing carts, platforms, also on wheels, to
keep the feet dry when getting off boats in a shallow
bottom ; the nurses and children ; the carriages and
liveries and flunkeys ; pony phaetons on hire, with
jockey boy riders, in striped silk costumes, astride
the horse, dash about everywhere, and add quite a
feature. Above all towers, story on story, and wide,

broad balcony on balcony, the enormous, overshad-
owing pile of the Grand Hotel.

There is an aquarium here, under ground, after
the style of the one at Brighton; but there is too
much to see in the air and sunlight that is fascinating, to waste any time on it.

Another stroll about Scarborough until noon, July 6.
when I return to Hull by a pleasant route through
Filey and Bridlington, passing near towns with the
familiar names of Beverly and Boston. V—— and
B—— arrive from London at three, and at six we
sail on the *Domino* for Norway. She is a clever
little steamer, of about 900 tons burthen, without
cargo and very light, — seeming a small bit of a
ship in contrast with the spacious accommodations
of the *Etruria.*

The passengers are all in the saloon at dinner-
time; but soon after getting outside the harbor we
begin to pitch and roll, to such an extent that very
few care to linger over the dessert; and very many
decide, quite early in the evening, that as we shall
probably lose a great deal of sleep during the weeks
of the voyage, they will turn in at once and get it
while they can!

July 7.　The North Sea seems determined to keep up its reputation, to-day at all events, and our wise friends of last evening seem equally determined to get their sleep while they may. A few of us have the breakfast tables entirely to ourselves, ditto lunch, ditto dinner. No wonder, for the motion is horrible! Mist and rain add to our discomfort. It is also cold and chilly. Altogether, a beastly day!

After nine, however, in the evening, a bright, clear, brilliant streak of color along the northern horizon, beneath the clouds, is a sure indication, Captain Tholander says, of fair weather to-morrow. This color continues all the evening, and is bright as ever when we go below at eleven.

STAVANGER.

July 8.　We sight the coast of Norway early, and soon after breakfast are amongst rocky islands, approaching the town of Stavanger, behind which, far inland, lie a long range of snow-capped mountains, blue and hazy in the morning mist. We moor alongside the pier at noon, and roam about the uninteresting little fishing village for a couple of hours, while our fresh provisions of salmon, lobster, milk and eggs are being put on board. At three we sail for Bergen, where we expect to arrive at midnight. The term is rather a misnomer in these latitudes, as already there are only a few hours of darkness left to us out of the twenty-four.

Our rough weather and sea-sickness are all over now for the rest of the voyage. We are in smooth water, inside of a vast chain of islands, which extend entirely along the coast. I think it would be almost literally true to here state (and I consider it my duty so to do, lest the description of our experience in crossing from the English to the Norwegian coast might deter some from making this cruise) that from this point north, with the exception of a few hours about the North Cape, we did not again see the open ocean, and that out of our large party of seventy-two, including many ladies, there was not another case of sea-sickness on board.

BERGEN.

We have an early breakfast, and spend the whole day on shore, dining at the Nord Hotel. The change from ship life was agreeable, and we passed a most enjoyable day. Next to Christiania, Bergen

July 9.

is the chief town of Norway. It is very pleasantly situated in a ravine, at the head of a long arm of the sea. A finely constructed roadway winds up a mountain side, near the town, which we slowly climbed for an hour, occasionally walking to relieve our plucky little, hardy pony. At every turn we had new and unsurpassed views of the valley below, the town, harbor, and fjord. The country is honeycombed with water in every direction, thus adding a striking feature to the vast panorama.

We drove inland four miles, up the valley, to see a curious old Norse church of fantastic architecture. It is one of several of its kind in Norway, built of hard pine, with a thick coat of black pitch in lieu of paint, reminding one somewhat of the eccentricities one sees in prints of Japanese structures. It was originally on the Sognefjord, but was purchased, brought to this place, and repaired by a private gentleman, simply to ornament his grounds. Its location is now superb : on a bold hill in the centre of a lovely valley, approached by well-kept walks, which lead to a succession of broad vistas of the surrounding country.

The peasants in their quaint costumes are interesting. We passed many of them during the day, either walking, driving in their tiny two-wheeled carts, or working in their curious, old-fashioned way on their little plots of ground. Let me give one illustration of their method of farm-work, — the hay-making. Poles are stuck in the ground in rows, between which are stretched parallel cords ; with their *hands* the green grass is gathered from the field, and is carefully bent and hung on these cords to dry ! This method of curing the grass was even used on the larger places, where it was cut with horses and an American mowing-machine.

After a stroll through the not very interesting museum, we sail northward at four, and must congratulate ourselves upon having had one of the few fair days of the year at Bergen.

ROMSDALS FJORD.

This is one of the many grand inlets, reaching far July 10. inland to the north of. Bergen. The approach and entrance this morning were delightful ; reminding one, in the way we were apparently closed in, at times, between the rocky walls, of sailing on The Lake of the Four Cantons, at Lucerne. We had a merry party on the forecastle after breakfast, betting on our course as we approached the different turning points.

At eleven, service was read by one of our passengers, a rector, — irreverently nicknamed "Three eyes," by some of our younger companions, from his English habit of wearing one eye-glass. The service was performed in such a matter-of-fact-way, and was so evidently a duty to be done and quickly over with, even to the stopping of the ship that we might not lose any of the scenery, that it might better have been entirely dispensed with : a great contrast to what one sees on the Atlantic, where the solemnity of the hour levels all ranks, and the crew, *en grande tenue*, officers, passengers, and emigrants, all assemble in the saloon on one common footing; where the captain would on no consideration waive his right to lead the service, and in a gruff, hearty, but reverent manner reads to the best of his ability. Nor shall I ever forget the memorable Sunday morning at sea when the Rev. Brooke Herford gave us one of his simple, noble, and impressive addresses.

Our service on the *Domino* was held in the so-called ball-room. As the cruise was entirely for the pleasure and comfort of the passengers, the unused forehold had very thoughtfully been cleanly painted, carpeted with white canvas, furnished with a piano and comfortable chairs and benches, and adorned with branches and green leaves. It made a large, useful room, which we used constantly for various purposes; where almost daily, after dinner, music and dancing were the order of the day.

We cast anchor after lunch, go ashore in our steam launch, and all take *carrioles* and *stolk* wagons up through the Romsdals Valley, around past the Romsdalshorn (which rises to a height of 5,090 feet), to the First Station. The scenery here is a repetition of that on the fjord, except that the valley walls close in about us, and the water is narrowed down to a noisy, turbulent, mountain torrent. The perpendicular walls of granite, several thousand feet high, with their barren sides, remind one of the Black Valley of the Gunnison in our Rockies. Snow lies on the tops and sides of all the peaks, extending down in many places to within a few feet of us, while clouds hang about the highest points. The roads are excellent, though of steep grades in places; but our rugged little Norwegian ponies are quite equal to it all.

At the First Station we halt. The more adventurous push on to the Second, some even to the Third Station, where they spend the night; but our immediate party preferred returning to our comfortable quarters aboard ship, to a good dinner, and to the quiet enjoyment of the grand spectacle of surrounding mountains and snow, as seen from the deck.

We have now, practically, daylight all night. It seems curious to hear good-nights taken, and to retire in the twilight; but sleep must be had, so we darken our staterooms and turn in.

July 11. What a lazily enjoyable life this is! Quite like my Mediterranean trip in my bachelor days of long ago. We have here no annoyance of luggage or customs; no expense of hotels; boats and a steam launch ply between ship and shore at all moments, and stewards are always at hand, always within call of an electric bell. We are in a floating hotel, in fact, which we take along with us wherever we go. Here in this far north country there is always much to interest one. Lounging in our sea chairs or chatting in groups, we have on all sides the grandest works of nature. Men are curing and gathering hay within sight, and at times only a few feet away from the snow and ice which melt and run down in fine streams or rapid torrents from the rocky mountain sides to the brawling rivers in the valleys, all to be gathered into the fjords on which we sail.

Leave at eleven for

MOLDE,

about an hour and a-half from our present anchorage, back and out towards the coast again.

We drive about on shore for three hours, above and beyond the town ; afterwards strolling under long rows of beech-trees to the Grand Hotel, where cakes and coffee were served on the verandah. A superb, bright day, with the same noble panorama of mountain and snow across the fjord, ever before us, whether walking or driving, whether on ship or shore.

We were awakened this morning by a dreadful July 12. din next our stateroom, and found that we were moored alongside the pier at

DRONTHEIM,

taking in coals. We escaped from the noise and dirt as soon as possible, taking refuge in Hotel d'Angleterre, where we found a crowding influx of two streams of tourists, from the north and south, taxed the resources of the establishment beyond all question of individual comfort.

Following the course of a river through and out beyond the town, during the forenoon, we drove about four miles back on the hills to a waterfall of some local renown. The water rushing down in great volumes, and dashing against rocks, fills the air with mist and spray, wetting every thing below and about, making the steep descent to the bottom very slippery, and the ascent most difficult.

Drontheim Cathedral, situated on the site of St. Olaf's well, is undergoing most thorough and extensive restoration. It is one of the oldest in Norway, and, aside from its really curious and interesting interior architecture, its marble octagon, gargoyles, carved heads and columns, it is within its sacred walls that every king of Norway must come for coronation.

The best view of the town and harbor is had from an old, dilapidated castle on the north side of the river. We spent most of the afternoon on its grass-grown walls. The vegetation of the valley is surprisingly green and luxuriant for the latitude, —

different from anything we have seen, or shall see again for some time.

The buildings, like all we have thus far seen in Scandinavia, are mostly of wood, with tile or stone roofs. They look new and modern for the traditions of the country, and are rather disappointing in this respect.

The inhabitants are cleanly, civil, honest, and obliging. The children are mostly pretty, the girls with bright red cheeks and light, flaxen hair. B—— forgot his coat, and left it — or rather I did — in a carriage at Veblungsnaes. As it was a new mackintosh, which he had just purchased in London, he took the trouble to go ashore on the chance of finding it. There stood the boy with it on the pier, waiting for him, much pleased at the opportunity of returning it. Fancy this of a coachman or cabby in most countries!

We lingered on deck last night, — or rather, this July 13. morning, for we no longer know day from night, — and for the first time saw the sun set and rise within thirty minutes. We did not at first realize what it was. We were all watching the sunset, — a deep crimson glow, — until gradually we noticed, only a

few points away, faint streaks of yellow light. We
thought at first a heavy cloud lay between, obstruct-
ing the color, until, with the rapidily increasing
light, we suddenly understood that we were watching the first break of dawn, while the deep crimson
of the sunset still lingered in the sky. At one
o'clock we went below, darkened our stateroom with
B——'s focussing cloth, and were soon asleep. This
morning when we got up we were at

TORGHATTEN,

65 deg. north latitude. This is an island, said to
resemble a hat; hence its name; but I failed to
make out the resemblance. It is a huge truncated
cone of rock, in the centre of which is a natural tunnel entirely through it. We landed in boats and
climbed up over the loose rocks and wet bogs to the
entrance of the shaft. It was a severe pull, but we
felt amply repaid. The tunnel is about sixty-five
feet high, and the same width, and five hundred feet
through. The rocks have fallen piece by piece, and
this makes the sharp descent a most difficult under-
taking. The view of the numerous islands and rocks,
as seen through this rocky square aperture, gave one

the impression of looking from a huge window in a tower.

Words will not describe the beauty of the evening July 14. and midnight hours last night. About eight the sun burst from a heavy cloud, bathing sea and mountain in a flood of light. The effect was superb as we all sat on the forecastle; the water was as smooth as glass, and the prow seemed to cut its way through a light skim of ice. The stillness was profound, and broken only by the noises of the ship. The light on the shore, mountain and snow was the most beautiful and peculiar that I have ever seen. Looking along shore to the north, it resembled a painting, with the bluish purple haze about the near mountains, fading to a grayish color, as the coast receded in the distance, while there was a flood of white crystal light on the snow, changing to a golden and later to a crimson glow. It was such a beautiful evening that the captain decided to go to the

SVARTISEN GLACIER,

about ten miles up one of the fjords. Here again was more good fortune for us. On his last trip this whole region was enveloped in fog, and nothing was

seen of this delightful neighborhood. We passed
the Seven Sisters after dinner, and the Arctic Circle
at 7.45. We landed about 11.30 P. M., at the foot of
the glacier, which here comes quite down to the sea.
As seen from the steamer, it appears only a few feet
away. Baedeker says it is seventy-eight miles long,
and one of the largest in the world. Of course, we
could only see a small portion of it as it lay glisten-
ing before us, rising up between two mountains
2,500 to 3,000 feet high. With great difficulty we
began a portion of its ascent. Walking upon it was
even perilous. The captain sent out with us six or
eight sailors with ropes and axes, and most useful
they were. In several places we could not go up
nor down without their aid and the steps they cut
for us. The contrasting dark blue and green colors
of the ice and water as seen away down the deep
fissures and crevasses were very beautiful in this
great frozen white sea. Hardy, thrifty, bright-colored
plants and flowers grew to the very glacier's edge.
We returned on board about one in the morning, a
weary but delighted party, to sit on the deck for another hour, watching the growing lights and colors of
the rising sun. A marvellous, wonderful experience is

this Arctic life and constant daylight! A dream never to be forgotten! After about six hours' sleep and a bath in the waters of the Arctic Ocean — clear, cold, and invigorating — we are again on deck, and find ourselves inside the Lafoten Islands, where, with clear weather, we hope to stop on our way back. The coast grows more bare and rugged, vegetation is more scarce, and we are in constant sight of snow. The day is clear and fine, warm on deck in the sun, and sleep is the order of the forenoon.

All day long we sail past huge granite boulders, July 15. covered with snow on top, and with sparse, greenish patches of moss lower down. Towards evening we pass through the fjord south of North Cape Island, and sail twenty-six miles to the eastward, to a point called Bird Island, under the north cliff of which we stop. A cannon was fired from the deck, and instantly the air was filled with millions on millions of birds. This is a vast breeding spot. Upon examining the wall with our glasses, we found every crack and crevice, every hole and projection, literally alive with birds and filled with nests, countless beyond description.

From this point we steamed back to the

NORTH CAPE,

the goal of all our northward travels. Entering and anchoring near a Norwegian excursion steamer, in a small bay on the east side, we landed about ten P. M., and began the steep, zigzag climb up the side of the rock, which is nearly 1,000 feet high. It was a most severe exertion, our inactive life aboard ship making it all the more difficult for us. My breath gave out at several places, my temples throbbed, and my head seemed filled to bursting. Up we climbed wearily, step by step, clinging to the ropes, — up, alongside a gorge filled with snow,—up, past bright double butter-cups (great balls of bright color on the grim walls), — up, past the pink, delicate blossoms of the green moss and the blue forget-me-nots, until, finally, wearied and worn out, we reached the level plateau and the glorious midnight sunlight. All our fatigue vanished in the enthusiasm of the hour. A longish walk over rough stones and through wet bog brought us to the monument commemorating the visit of King Oscar II., and to the edge of the cliff, — the northernmost point of one continent. The weather was superb. There was not a cloud in the sky, and, at midnight, the sun was still ten degrees above the horizon. Geiger raised his American flag, which he had carried with him for 40,000 miles in a tour around the world, and which he had flung to the breeze on the Pyramids, on the Chinese Wall, in the vale of Cashmere, and away up among the Himalayas. Our boatswain and sailors raised the English colors. We drank to the rulers of America, of England, and of Norway, and shout after shout went up as the different toasts were proposed. Away, far to the north of us, stretched the Arctic Ocean. We were many miles to the north of the corresponding latitude in which Sir John Franklin lost his life, and within about eighteen degrees of the North Pole. B—— photographed the rock, the sun, and our group, all between twelve and one A. M. After our excitement had abated a bit, we sat down to enjoy one of the unique moments of our lives. Away, far, far below us, lay our steamer. There was water in front, and on both sides of us, and behind us the stern, forbidding rocks. We sat and gazed away up northward, while our thoughts and feelings were too deep for conversation. Not a syllable was spoken until, with a deep sigh, we realized that we must up and away again.

The return to our launch and ship was most reluctantly made; but, all the way down, the panorama of bay and path and rocks below us was most enjoyable. The passengers, descending in long files and zigzag lines, clinging to the ropes, looked like tiny ants in the distance. The ladies could not resist plucking the flowers within their reach as they passed along,—reminding one of the way cows crop the last mouthful of sweet green grass along the roadside as they are being driven home. We reached the ship about two A. M., and then went for a couple of hours' fishing. About four we steamed away, this time to the south, for Hammerfest and the beginning of our homeward journey.

HAMMERFEST,

July 16. the northernmost town in Europe, is not noted for cleanliness or its objects of interest.

We saw Lapps for the first time, male and female; greasy, dirty-looking creatures they are! There was an amusing incident in front of one of the wooden curio shops this morning. A Lapp girl had been following our party about the village for some time, apparently—except that she moved on when we did, and stopped when we stopped — stolid and indifferent to every thing. Not a muscle of her face ever altered from its wooden stare. The ladies wagered that I could not bring a smile to her face. I went down off the rickety wooden steps to the street, smiling kindly and approaching closely to try and awaken some interest in her; but all to no avail. She stood as indifferent as an aged but faithful mastiff, who cannot be persuaded to move on until his master goes. At last I took out a silver kroner and put it in her hand. Suddenly she smiled all over, a broad, coarse smile of delight, and, putting out her huge paw, I was obliged to submit to a regular pump-handle hand-shake, in thanks for my colossal present to her. The shrieks of laughter, the clapping of hands and shouts of amusement from our party, made a din which filled the whole narrow street, under cover of which I retired to wash my hands!

The town is small, and entirely unimportant. We forcibly recalled what Captain Tholander said of Stavanger, as we were approaching it in the early part of our voyage: 'There is nothing to see, and I shall give you plenty of time to see it in.'

On the way out of the harbor, we saw on our right the famous Meridian Stone.

We sailed at noon, and for several hours experienced cold, foggy, raw weather, which chilled us to the bone ; but later we had the benefit of it in a fresh layer of clean, beautiful snow, which covered every peak and mountain - top about us. By eight P. M. the weather cleared, so that on reaching

TROMSÖ,

at midnight, the sun was shining bright and clear. We anchored in the middle of the fjord, opposite the town, which is built up and back on the hill from the water. As this will be our last sight of the Midnight Sun, — probably, in my case at least, forever, we could not turn in. So, with a couple of the officers, five of us rowed ashore, where we strolled about, through and above the town, climbing the hill back of it, and getting fine views of the fjord and islands, old Sol gloriously shedding his golden light all the while.

At three in the morning we rowed back on board, and turned in ; but, alas ! not to sleep. While I like nothing better, and never sleep sounder than at sea, on the other hand there is nothing more disgustingly uncomfortable than a night at anchor. All ventilation is stopped, the staterooms are hot, every sound and footstep is magnified in the quiet of rest and stillness on board ; and every one who has been to sea knows that the shovelling of coals, dumping of ashes, pumping of water for washing down the decks, and other sundry details of ships' keeping, need no magnifying.

However, a good fresh bath at seven refreshed and rested us, so that after breakfast we started out in good trim for the Lapp and reindeer settlements up the mountains. July 17.

V—— and I drove in state, with a pair of courageous little ponies, two native drivers, and a whole retinue of men and children, Russian Finns, and Lapps, of both sexes. We should have enjoyed the drive, had we not been in such constant and imminent danger of upsetting. For most of the distance our drivers, by main strength, held up our sundown (!) as we rattled and slid sidewise up and down the mountain-sides.

At last we reached the camp and our friends, who had all preceded us on foot and horseback. They were all having a photograph taken in the reindeer enclosure.

We were disappointed in the size of the camp and the scarcity of the Lapps ; but as we had been meeting them occasionally for several days, and had become pretty well accustomed to the dirty, filthy creatures, it did not much matter. They are low of stature,—in fact, dwarfed and stunted in appearance, —and unclean beyond description. Their fur garments holding and even breeding vermin to such an extent that one reluctantly walked about the grounds occupied by them. Their earthen huts are even worse than their persons ! A herd of about fifty reindeer were noble in comparison with them, with their wide-spreading antlers. The snapping of the knee-joints, without Baedeker's hint, we should have supposed to be the rattling together of their long hoofs. Despite their clumsiness, they are gracefully formed. I would like to see a herd of them in their native state dashing across a mountain ravine!

After lunch B——— and I make another trip to town, and at four we weigh anchor for the South again.

A few days more and we leave the good ship's

company; reluctantly enough we do it, too. Life on an excursion like the present is very different from the etiquette of an Atlantic steamer. We are in the midst of the grand works of nature, and a common feeling of irresistible enthusiasm and elation at finally reaching a spot, for the first time, that has always been a bright dream of a golden future, awakens and develops rapidly a kindred feeling of good-fellowship and *camaraderie* which seems to make old and good friends in a few days' time, and which is rapidly kindled by one common interest and the welfare of the whole, by each individual. The ship becomes a comfortable refuge and home. It is often with a sigh of satisfaction and relief that we catch sight of her quietly riding at anchor, after a wearisome tramp and a tiresome side journey on shore. The officers — yes, even the sailors of our crew — are a welcome sight to us.

This morning when we woke we found we were away up the Rafsund, and amongst the July 18.

LAFOTEN ISLANDS.

The scenery is grand, the pointed rocks rising high above and around us; but we have become to a certain extent satiated with grandeur in Nature, and the impressions were not what they would have been earlier in the voyage. At places we passed between lofty walls scarcely wide enough for the steamer. In its way, this is all quite different from the coast scenery; but it comes a bit too late for our fullest enjoyment of it. It is a glorious day as we drift slowly and lazily about, from one headland to another, passing numerous fishing villages.

It is a most indolent way of sight-seeing, stretched comfortably on our favorite perch in the forecastle with our merry, congenial party about one, passing through a slowly moving and double panorama of magnificent scenery, in a mild, warm, bright sunshine; gazing about from the deep blue water beneath us up to the hoary peaks and the snow-fields, which no longer excite our enthusiasm. A lazy, dreamy, delightful languor, which we know cannot last, but to which knowledge we give no thought; happy and content, dreaming of the loved ones at home; indolently comfortable, with as complete a feeling of *dolce far niente* as ever the Southern lands can give.

So passed a whole bright summer's day, with an

extensive mirage for hundreds of miles along the horizon toward evening, to which even we gave but too scanty attention, accustomed as we have become in these glorious weeks to the grand and the wonderful.

A cold, misty, dreary day, which makes us more reconciled to leave the ship. Impossible to keep warm, or to remain on deck. The smoke-room crowded. July 19.

Toward night, the Crown Prince of Sweden, with his wife, on a Norwegian steamer with flags and banners flying from every mast, overtake and pass us in a narrow passage. They sail proudly, but carelessly, by. If we had not slowed down, there would have been a collision.

At dinner, Captain made a most complimentary speech, regretting our departure on the morrow. Three rousing cheers were given, and all, rising, joined in the chorus, "For they are jolly good fellows," etc. It was a very pleasant occasion, and only a repetition and another expression of the courtesy and good-fellowship with which our countrymen are received by their English cousins across the water.

DRONTHEIM.

July 20.　Our party of fourteen, all Americans, leave the ship early, and start by train at eight A. M. for Stockholm. Captain, officers, and many of the passengers accompany us to the station, where they give us a good send-off, — cheering as the train rolled out of the building.

At the Swedish border we succeed in getting a through special car, with staterooms and connecting corridor. A jolly party we are! V—— has some new joke at every station. At times he is inimitable, with an inexhaustible fund of humor. The natives will remember the passage of our car for many a day, and the noisy mirth of its occupants.

July 21.　Another day in the cars, travelling through Sweden. Miles and miles of birch and pine forests.

We lunched at Upsala. At the railway restaurants in Scandinavia there are no waiters. Food is placed on a large central table, from which travellers help themselves, choosing, as their fancy dictates, from a bounteous and well-cooked supply. Payment is made at the door in passing out. A fixed price of so much each, without reference to the quantity consumed or the variety of selection.

We had a good view of the University Building and grounds, with its numerous branch colleges scattered about over the village. Over all, towers on a hill in the centre a large, ugly, but conspicuous, red-brick castle. We reached

STOCKHOLM

at four, having been thirty-two consecutive hours in making a journey of not over five hundred miles! We spend the evening strolling and steaming in small boats about the city in the long twilight, dining on an open verandah in one of the numerous concert gardens. How delicious that dinner tasted after our weeks at sea, and how we did enjoy it, listening to the strains of Mettra's 'La Rose,' Auber, Meyerbeer, Rossini, Beethoven, Verdi, Wagner, and Gounod!

The city is composed of islands, connected by bridges, lying between the Baltic and Lake Malaren. At high tide the water is salt, from the sea; at low tide it is fresh, from the lake. Steam launches dart swiftly about in every direction, taking the place of coach and omnibus. In the gardens, standard rosebushes grow to the size of small trees, blossoming

profusely. The neatness and cleanliness of the
Swedes is everywhere noticeable, — in the streets,
buildings, cars and carriages; on the quays and
boats.

We are all at the Grand Hotel, — a fine building,
centrally and beautifully located, facing the water.
It was from one of its balconies that Nilsson sang
years ago, when twenty-three persons lost their lives
in the crush in the square below.

We are already enchanted with the city, and can
readily understand why a lady at the hotel, who came
to spend a few days, has lingered for three weeks.

July 22-24.   Three memorable days at Stockholm, in this gay-
est of all gay cities, Paris not excepted! One's
recollections are of music everywhere; of steaming
from one island to another in the swift little boats;
of dining in summer gardens down by the very
water's edge, or on heights giving panoramic views
of sea and shore, with always a performance to watch
or music to listen to all the while.

Thanks to our letters of introduction to gentlemen
here, some one of whom has always been with us, to
their generous hospitality and kindly entertainment,
we have seen the city and its sights to the best

advantage, visited the best places at the best times, and economized our moments in every way.

At this season of the year the short hours of the night are like a long twilight, and it is the favorite time for driving. We were taken entirely around one of the larger islands one night, not starting until after twelve, lunching at a charming little house by the sea at one, and having a glorious sunrise, on our way back, between two and three o'clock in the morning.

The pleasant companionship of our large party ends on the last of these three days, with a farewell dinner-party at Hasselbacken, after which V——, B ——, and I leave by train for Copenhagen. I shall return again for a few days ; but to most of us beautiful Stockholm is another dream of the past. How inadequate language is to describe such a city ; and how impossible it is to put in words our enjoyment of it !

Travelling all night in a Swedish sleeping-car, July 25. —the wide beds and fresh linen sheets of such scrupulous neatness that it was a pleasure to occupy and use them, —we arrived at Malmö, through the most fertile and cultivated part of the peninsula that we have seen, at eight A. M., and cross by boat to

COPENHAGEN,

arriving at Hotel d'Angleterre about half-past ten. We immediately took carriages, and had a busy day, driving about the city and environs, over broad avenues, between rows of the dark, heavy foliage of the beech-tree: a fertile, interesting country, with picturesque windmills here and there, reminding one not a little of Holland.

The citadel, surrounded by a moat, overhanging which trees and bushes have been allowed to grow in wild profusion, is open and free to all. Indeed, a central passage-way through it seems to be used as a public thoroughfare, both for walking and driving.

Outside and around the citadel, on the harbor side, is the so-called Lange Linie, a broad promenade and delightful resort, giving good, unobstructed views out over the water. The Cattegat is to-day more crowded with shipping than I have ever seen the English Channel, and the port of Copenhagen is a busy place, with its protecting squadron of grey ironclads.

The architecture of some of the buildings is very

quaint and curious. One church spire, apparently
of greenish bronze, has an external spiral staircase
coiling up about it to a globe on the top, on which
is a colossal human figure. The handsome façade
of the low-domed opera-house is surmounted by a
spirited bronze group of 'Victory' driving her chariot,
designed by Thorwaldsen. The whole city speaks
on every side of the great master : I never realized
before *how* great. In the Fruekirke are his colossal
figures of 'Christ' (a copy of which we saw in Drontheim Cathedral) and the 'Twelve Apostles.'

The Thorwaldsen Museum is, of course, the main
object of interest. It is in the shape of a mausoleum,
on the exterior and interior walls of which are frescoes of events in the artist's life. It contains all his
creations, either originals, or duplicates in plaster.
His versatility was wonderful, and it is difficult to
believe that the same hand and brain that produced
the colossal equestrian statue of 'Maximilian I.,' at
Munich, or the 'Dying Lion of Lucerne,' fashioned
the exquisitely graceful and delicate reliefs of 'Day'
and 'Night' and the 'Ages of Love.'

Several rooms in the building contain part of his
furniture, library, pictures, and antiquarian collec-

tions. The paintings are not worthy of mention, but the scarabæ, coins, and Etruscan pottery are most interesting and valuable.

The museum is built about a hollow square, or quadrangle, in the centre of which is his grave, simply marked by a bed of dark green ivy. It is the only color or life to break the simplicity of the enclosure of walls and pavement. But no headstone is necessary: his noble monument is all about him, and his living marble figures speak for him.

Unfortunately, many of the artisans at Copenhagen, taking advantage of the fame and reputation of their great sculptor's works, and of the avidity with which many travellers will buy, as souvenirs, cheap reproductions, have filled every shop-window, hotel, and restaurant in the city with terra cotta and Parian cupids, graces, dying lions, etc., with a surfeiting profusion.

I leave at 6.30 P. M. by return boat for Malmö and Sweden. As I now write in the smoke-room of the little steamer, the panorama of the Zealand coast is rapidly fading away in the golden halo of the setting sun. V—— and B—— I have left behind. They start in the morning for Paris, and I am alone for the first time since leaving New York. As I think of it, and of all the busy, jolly, happy, enjoyable days we have had together, it is difficult to overcome my lonely feelings. But Russia and Moscow lie before me!

A tiresome all-night ride by rail (changing cars at three o'clock in the morning), without being able to get much rest or sleep, made a quiet day at July 26.

GOTHENBURG

very welcome. In the afternoon I very unexpectedly met a party of friends. We drove in the environs for a couple of hours, and then dined together at the Horticultural Gardens. At ten in the evening I left on the little canal steamer *Baltsar Von Platen.*

THE GOTHA CANAL.

Had an early tramp, before breakfast, to see the Trolhatta Falls, of such great renown in Sweden. They are simply a turbulent, mad rush of waters, in whirlpools and rapids, down through a rocky gorge, —picturesque, but scarcely worth a special trip. As is often the custom on these boats, we had taken advantage of the time consumed in passing through July 27.

a series of locks to make a side excursion on shore.
We easily stepped on board again at the little town
of Trolhatta, where we had arranged with our captain to meet. Each lock is 105 feet long, and raises
or lowers about ten feet every time it is opened or
closed. The craft that pass through cannot measure
over 103 feet. Fancy making a trip across lakes and
country, from Gothenburg to Stockholm, in such
a little tub! And yet, we were surprisingly comfortable. We crossed Lake Venern, ninety miles long,
and, towards evening, again entered the canal and
began lock-work. It was a curious sensation to sit
on the upper deck of a steamer, and feel the soft,
easy motion of the propeller under one's feet, while
looking out immediately on wilderness or farm. At
times the canal lay through a dense forest, cutting
its way, straight as a die, between the trees for miles
and miles. As the boat nearly filled the width of the
canal, and the trees grew to its very edge, there was
no water to be seen, and the delusion was complete.

As the boat was behind time, and I wanted to
catch the night train at Toreboda, there was no
help for it but to take a horse and wagon at one
o'clock in the morning, and drive for an hour across

country in the dark, with a total stranger, who could
not speak a word of English : a thing I should hesitate to do in many countries, of which honest Sweden is not one.

STOCKHOLM.

Spent the forenoon in arranging my passage on July 28.
the Swedish steamer *Finland*, for St. Petersburg via
Finland. The proper visé of one's passport by the
Russian consul is the first and most absolutely necessary step, for without it one cannot even purchase a
ticket on any boat sailing for Russia. It is given
up to the agents upon payment of the fare, handed
by them to the captain, who returns it, after a second
visé by Finnish officials, *en route*. Here again my
letters of introduction in Stockholm became useful
for the purpose of identification before the consul.
As a souvenir of a trip to Russia, — what with the
endorsements of permission to enter, to reside in
each of the cities visited, and finally to leave the
country, — one's passport, with the various official
stamps and signatures, becomes the most curious
that one can have.

After all of this red tape had been satisfactorily
attended to, I gained admission to the Historical

Museum of Stockholm. Baedeker does well to mark
it with two stars. It is the most instructive and
interesting collection it has ever been my good fortune to examine. The Flint and Bronze Periods,
and the Iron Age, are all chronologically arranged.
There is also a Mediæval room, and a large assort-
ment of coins.

With a professor of the building constantly ex-
plaining, I spent two interesting hours in the various
rooms, beginning with the Flint Period, before metals
were known, carefully examining a very large and
excellent collection of stone implements and flint
weapons. It was most fascinating and instructive
to follow the development from the rude stone ham-
mers of prehistoric times to the gradual introduction
of the metals; then, as civilization advanced and
luxuries were indulged in, bronze ornaments and
adornments were seen: at first rude and clumsy,
then of finer workmanship, till rings and horse trappings began to appear, and finally gold and precious
stones, mosaic work, *cloisonné*, and so on down to
wood carvings, paintings, etc., and the minute
perfection of modern times.

In the afternoon I went out over Lake Malaren,

with its twelve hundred islands, to Drottingsholm, one of the royal villas. The lake is so cut up and filled with bits of wooded land, that it has the appearance of a succession of bays and inlets, which convey no impression of a continuous sheet of water.

In the evening, went for one more round of the concert gardens, dining at Mosebacken, to enjoy the panorama of city and water once more. Ah, how I do regret leaving this *queen* of cities! Life here is all a dream of pleasure, with music at every turn.

The best band is Steiner's Hungarian (Buda-Pesth), composed of about thirty boys, from nine to eighteen years of age. The Kapellmeisters' control is perfect; their playing is most inspiriting. I have rarely heard such rendering of all kinds of music.

Stockholm is a paradise for the telephone. There are two companies, one of them with over six thousand subscribers. Every house and shop has them both, even to the small, corner retailers. Many of the boats have them in their officers' room; as soon as they arrive at their berth, connection is made over the side of the ship with the system. In shopping, if a stranger cannot understand a shopkeeper, all he has to do is to call up his hotel-porter, and make his bargain through him by telephone. The numerous wires are very small and fine. They are no obstruction to the roofs, or in case of fire, as they are carried high in the air, over huge structures, which are in themselves objects of curiosity to the stranger.

Prices are most reasonable, and the cost of living very low: a ride in the street cars entirely around the city for two and a half cents; an hour's ride by steamer over the lake for twenty-five cents; my room at the Grand Hotel, as fine a building as most of the larger hotels in Paris, and delightfully located, for eighty-seven and a half cents a day; a dinner, with French cooking, of six courses, at the best restaurant, for thirty-seven and a half cents, and everything in this same proportion.

We sail at midnight. The city, with its countless lights over water and hill, fades gradually away in the moonlight; but the memories of beautiful Stockholm are ours forever more; and like the drink at the Fountain of Trevi in Rome, once indulged in, one is sometime sure to return.

Crossing the Gulfs of Bothnia and Finland, in a
crowded steamer, with poor accommodations and
wretched food.   At three P. M. we reach

ABÖ,

in Finland, and for the first time see the striped red,
white, and blue flag waving over Russian soil.   We
moor alongside the hot, noisy pier, and submit to
the customs' examination of our luggage (although
none of it is taken ashore), and have our passports
examined and endorsed by the police.   The waiting
hours are only relieved by a visit to the prison, —
an interesting, but certainly not a very cheering,
experience.   We were taken through many different
rooms and workshops, where prisoners were busily engaged at their various trades.   Everywhere through-
out the building, upon our approach, they rose and
remained standing while in our presence.   We peeped
at those in solitary confinement, through small eye-
holes in the doors.   They all seemed brutish animals ;
showing, with but one exception, no sign of intel-
ligence.   This one stared at us through a pair of
large glasses with his whole soul.   His black eyes
haunt me still !

HELSINGFORS.

July 30.   Visited the Russian (Greek) Church, under whose
lofty dome we first saw the Icon, with which we soon
became so familiar in the weeks that followed. It
is a very tall altar-screen, in many cases extending
quite up into the dome, of finest gold gilding, with
panelled rows, one above another, of paintings of
various saints, patrons, and royal personages. In
marked contrast to all this display of gold, marble,
and color, was the interior of the Lutheran Cathedral, — plain even to bareness, with no ornamentation
whatever to break the stern, almost forbidding, aspect of the walls and ceiling.

A comfortable dinner in a garden restaurant, with
a long walk through the grounds afterward, occupied
the afternoon until our ship sailed. We then had
two delightful hours on deck : the blue and gold
towers and minarets of the principal buildings giving
us our first taste of Russian architecture, while we
sat listening, until far out to sea, to the sweet
music of the bronze and silver bells ringing in answering cadences from every tower and church in
the town.

The fortifications on all the shore and islands,

which even at this distance from the capital begin
to defend the approach to its port, are most extensive
and mysterious.

At sunset we saw what in the darkness of a cold
winter's night in this latitude I should describe as
an aurora borealis: great pencils or shafts of light
and shadow radiating from the sun over one-half of
the heavens, spreading out in an immense fan shape,
like the spread of a peacock's tail.

WIBORG.

This is the nearest port to the great Finnish Falls, July 31.
which a Russian gentleman on board soberly assured
us were, next to Niagara, the largest and grandest
in the world. We did not visit them, notwithstand-
ing this tempting (!) statement, but took advantage
of our early arrival to breakfast on shore. The cool,
quiet room of a restaurant, pleasantly situated on a
hill-top, was delicious and enjoyable after the crush
and scrambling for food in the noisy saloon of our
steamer. We enjoyed our good coffee, omelet, and
strawberries all the more when thinking of the pork
chops we had left behind.

Sailed again at eleven, and now we are really off

for Russia, where we shall drink the famous caravan tea, — the first we have ever tasted that has not crossed an ocean.

Passed an arm of the gulf at noon, which, to our surprise, contained some twenty or more Russian men-of-war and torpedo boats. Two or three of them were of immense size, and all swarming with 'navvies.' As we approach St. Petersburg, our respect for the Empire of the North grows with every league we travel.

Cronstadt comes into sight about six P.M., bristling with guns. Batteries and earthworks on every island, and on either shore, form a circle of defense about the mouth of the Neva. The masts of men-of-war, ironclads, torpedo boats, and training-ships, through which we pass, seem like a forest.

From Cronstadt up the river, through breakwaters on either side forming a broad canal in the middle of the stream, one spire after another appears gleaming in the sunlight. First of all, the grand dome of St. Isaac's Cathedral; then the needle-like golden shaft of the Admiralty Building; and, most beautiful of all, the blue central dome, with its four satellites, of the Church of the Trinity, glittering with golden stars. We passed Peterhof, with its Summer Palaces, and arrived at

ST. PETERSBURG

about eight in the evening. The long-dreaded customs' examination proved, as I have always elsewhere found it to be, a mere matter of form. The searching and severe examination and confiscation by the Russian government officials had been so exaggerated, in all the accounts that I had read and been told of, that before leaving Sweden I had seriously thought of sending my photographs, books, and curios home by express. The only severity I experienced was in having my luggage overhauled *twice*. This was due to the very short memory of the man assigned to me. His Sunday libations (the vice of all the lower classes in Russia) had been too often repeated during the day, fortunately for me; for it was the cause of teaching me, on first landing, the useful and most important secret of comfort in getting about, and avoidance of difficulties with officials in this country; namely, to yield to all their demands, however unreasonable or unjust: a lesson which I remembered, and which was exceedingly valuable on a later occasion. In the present instance,

when I began to remonstrate and attempt to explain
that my trunks had but just been examined and were
already labelled, the quiet and timely hint of a courteous hotel interpreter, to let the man have his own
way and all would be well, without any doubt saved
some of my books at least from the confiscation I
had feared.

On the other hand, the examination and scrutiny
of one's passport is most careful and thorough.
No bribing, yielding, or hope of leniency in this
matter will be of any avail to the unfortunate
traveller whose credentials are not perfect, and absolutely in conformity with the law in every respect.
Within two years, our captain told us, one of his
passengers who had neglected a trifling requirement
had not been allowed to land, and had been obliged
to spend the whole ten days of the ship's stay at St.
Petersburg on board ; sailing away with him on his
return trip, without ever having set foot in the city,
in the very midst of which he lay moored, and which
he had travelled fifteen hundred miles to see.

Later, when preparing to leave, in order to save
time I had my *visé pour l'étranger* done at Moscow.
At St. Petersburg, where this visé is usually obtained

when leaving from that port, it is customary to receive a duplicate, on a separate piece of paper, which
is kept by the examining official who boards all ships
at Cronstadt, on their way out of the harbor. This
duplicate I did not have, and was promptly informed
that I could not leave the country ; but must return
with them to the city, with all my belongings. As
there was not another sailing for England for a week,
my connection with the Atlantic steamer on which
I had arranged to leave for home depended entirely
on my getting away without delay ; and I put the
case so strongly to him that at last, with great con-
descension, he unwillingly agreed to send ashore for
higher authority. For one hour my fate hung in the
balance, while our captain fretted and fumed at the
delay. At last 'his highness' arrived in a government launch with flying colors and uniformed crew,
listened to my explanation (how devoutly I blessed
my old tutor for drilling the French verbs into my
dull brains !), critically examined the visé, and in a
dignified manner directed his subalterns to make
a copy ; and the fiat came forth, at last, that I
could depart.

All this digression is simply to impress upon any

one of my readers, who may contemplate a journey
to Russia, the absolute importance and necessity
of obtaining full and complete information of passport requirements, and to rigidly attend to the
carrying out and careful execution of the same.
After getting our luggage from the quay, F——
and I drove to Hotel de l'Europe, on the Newski
Prospect. We engaged our rooms, then at once
took a droski for the Zoölogical Gardens, — a summer resort on one of the islands on the northern
side of the river, — where we had dinner, watched
a ballet (Last Days of Pompeii), went to the theatre,
and stared at the crowd. The droski is a most absurd little vehicle, without rail or protection about
the seat ; and there is constant danger, as one is
being driven along at a speed of ten or twelve miles
an hour, of being thrown out into the street. The
drivers have long coats, with flowing skirts, belted
in at the waist, and a most curiously shaped, little,
low-crowned, stiff hat.

The Neva is a broad, rapid stream, averaging
nearly half a mile in width. The Troitzki Bridge,
which crosses it from the Summer Gardens, is of
wood, resting on pontoons, which are taken up in

winter. We were four minutes in driving rapidly and nine minutes in walking across. Like everything else in the capital, its size is its extraordinary feature. The vast, sweeping views from it, in either direction, and on both sides of the river, of quays, buildings, façades, spires, domes, and towers, are unparalleled. St. Petersburg is truly an imperial city! To quote again from Baedeker, 'The expenditure of space is magnificent'! No idea of the size and extent of the buildings, squares, streets, and bridges can be given; for there is nothing in the world to compare them with. The architecture is neither technically fine nor attractive; but one marvels at measurements and acreage. I will give but one example, the Winter Palace, whose walls are 450 by 350 feet. It is a long walk across Alexander Square from it to the Triumphal Arch; while the length of these and the surrounding frontages, when first seen, arrest one's steps, and one stares in amazement.

By the Julian calendar we have lost twelve days; July 20, consequently, while in the Russian Empire we must (Aug. 1.) use a double date. Three hours to-day in the Hermitage, amongst paintings, statuary, and antiquities.

The galleries are rich in paintings, and many *chefs d'œuvres* are here found which one misses in the collections of old masters in Paris, Dresden, and Central Europe: notably a superb collection of Murillo's sacred subjects; Rembrandt's 'Sacrifice of Abraham' and 'Descent from the Cross;' Titian's 'Danaë' and 'Toilette de Vénus;' Quentin Metsy's 'Misers;' Gerard Dow's 'Own Portrait;' the finest set of Snyder's game pictures that I know of; many old Dutch paintings, appropriately framed in flat black wood. The sculptures are unimportant. The Hermitage Venus is in perfect preservation, but sadly disappointing. Even in this brief and totally inadequate hint of a few of the best known and most celebrated works of The Hermitage, I cannot omit to mention the Kertch collection, with its superb gold, silver, and bronze ornaments. F——, an Oxford graduate and professor, who has made the study of classics the business of his life, pronounces it the finest and most interesting collection of its kind he has yet met with. His whole day has been spent in it.

The entrance to the Hermitage is unique. Ten colossal human figures, of dark marble, support the *porte-cochère*, and form a most imposing approach. Passing inside the doors, the staircase and two-storied entrance hall take away one's breath in admiring wonder! At the second story, on either side of the stairway, rows of huge, dark granite columns support the lofty roof. The effect of distance, of size, of lofty ceiling and enclosed space, is grand and imposing in the extreme. In the corridor, at the top of this flight of steps, fabulous tables, huge vases, candelabra and urns of malachite and of lapis lazuli, dazzle one. It all reminded me very forcibly of a conversation I once heard in a cosmopolitan hotel in Italy. An American had just bought a small malachite ring, with which he was immensely pleased; showing it to all about, and expecting the customary admiration, which almost every one expressed. One man, a Russian, said not a word. Pressed by the American to take some notice of it, he finally said: 'Yes, very pretty, very pretty. I have a mantel - piece of the same at home'! I thought him a brute at the time; I do not now. The stone was as common a sight to him as the finer grades of polished marbles with which we decorate our best buildings are to us.

One room of The Hermitage contains a wax figure of Peter the Great, many of his tools, lathes, desks, canes, a wagon, and, under a glass case, his favorite horse and dogs, stuffed for preservation. In the afternoon and evening we drove, making the *Tour des Isles,* stopping at the Round Point to see the celebrated view of the sunset out over the waters of the Gulf. These islands form pleasant and fashionable suburbs, with numerous charming summer residences nestling amongst the trees, close by the water; looking very inviting with their open, furnished verandahs and surrounding grounds. Finished the evening at the Aquarium Gardens; again walking home across the wooden bridge and down the promenade by the Neva, in front of the Public Buildings. What a panorama! the distant and interminable rows of light on quay and bridge, the rapid river, the long façades, the golden domes, towers, and thin, needle-like spires; above all, the brilliant full moon. We can imagine the scene in winter! one great frozen sea of ice and snow, covered with skaters circling about; the sleighs with their furs and gay trappings; the life, the activity, and the splendor of it all!

A day in churches, beginning with that of Kasan
on the Newski Prospect, with its massive silver
ornamentation, its Virgin with a diamond crown,
and its semi-circular arcades in ridiculous imitation
of St. Peter's.

The wealth and magnificence of St. Isaac's Cathedral is peculiar to itself. Ten large columns of fluted
malachite, thirty feet high, with two of lapis lazuli
in the centre, support and divide the choir and
altar from the nave! Numberless huge monoliths
of polished Finnish granite, at least six feet in
diameter, support the outside porticoes on each
side, with steps and pavement of the same material.
The capitals, bases, and pedestals of all these columns,
both inside and outside of the structure, and the
huge exterior circular railing around the base of the
upper dome, are all of bronze. The entrance doors
and the greater part of the ceilings, which are adorned
with colossal figures in high relief, are also of bronze;
together with the delicate open-work screen altar-
doors, which are fire gilded. Immense mosaics of
saints and apostles adorn the walls; and a colossal
copy of the 'Last Supper,' also in mosaic, is now
being placed above the altar doors. A stained

window behind the altar, representing a figure of the Saviour, must be at least fifty feet high. Numberless swinging candelabra, of massive silver, hang before shrines in various parts of the cathedral, of a size to correspond with the vast interior. There are several Bible covers and shrine screens, thirty to forty inches square, of gold, adorned with numberless rubies, amethysts, diamonds, and other precious stones. In the altar, behind the screen, is a reproduction in detail of the building, about three feet square, of gold. This is a bare statement of a part of the treasures and adornments of this great structure, the effects of which are enhanced tenfold by their position and combinations. In its way, it is as imposing as St. Peter's or Milan Cathedral. There is not that detail of finish, the lines of architectural and sculptural beauty, to dazzle the eye; but a colossal and massive impressiveness of wall and column that remind one of the Baalbec and Egyptian structures, together with a lavish costliness of material which only the mines and quarries of Siberia and Finland can supply.

We climbed to the top, and were well repaid with a comprehensive — in fact, the only good — view of

St. Petersburg, the Neva, islands, suburbs, and harbor that can be had.

The cottage once occupied by Peter the Great is protected by a building constructed over and about it. It contains desks and furniture, together with the famous boat (the grandfather of the Russian navy), all made by the great Emperor's own hands. The house is now used as a shrine. We found it filled with devout people who bowed their foreheads to the very pavement in the sincerity of their worship. This we have noticed to be an universal custom amongst the natives at prayer, reminding one of the Eastern prostration.

The church of SS. Peter and Paul, in the Old Arsenal, is the Pantheon of Russia. It contains the remains of all the Imperial Family since the days of Peter the Great. Plain, simple, white marble sarcophagi, in different parts of the church, enclosed by railings, and marked only with bronze tablets. Battle flags are arranged about the columns of the structure, which is guarded by soldiers.

We saw a capital representation of the 'Mikado,' in Russian, at the Livardia Garden Theatre. During the summer months, in Russia, these numerous gardens are the favorite resort after the heat of the day. They are attractively laid out, with extensive grounds, band-stand, open-air stage, restaurant, and theatre. Numerous small tables and chairs, with waiters in attendance, are scattered about everywhere, in front of the various performances and under the trees. The play in the theatre, for which an additional admission is charged, continues through the evening, with numerous long *entr'actes*, during which the entire audience leave the building to stroll about the grounds, take refreshments or drink, listen to the band, or watch the smaller side performances, until the ringing of a bell notifies them to return again to the theatre for another act.

From the performance of the 'Mikado,' we returned to the English Quay, at midnight, by one of the express boats on the Neva, going around the islands in the moonlight. We never can cross the river without outspoken admiration of the magnificent, sweeping panorama, each time discovering some new feature. One can watch the driving and the pedestrians on quays and bridges for hours.

July 22, (Aug. 3.) This is the fête day of the Empress. Attended service in the morning at Smolna Cathedral, which

is surrounded by immense cloisters. The services
were conducted with great pomp by Monseigneur
Isidor, the *Métropolitain* (head of the Greek Church
at St. Petersburg), assisted by the Archbishop
and other high church dignitaries, whose robes
of gold thread and gold lace were most sumptuous.
The daughters of the nobility are educated here.
They were all present in their different convent costumes, with their teachers and attendants ; many of
the older governesses wore decorations.

As the venerable *Métropolitain* came out, after the
services, to his white satin-lined coach, which was
drawn by four black stallions, with postillions and
footmen, a vast crowd assembled near the steps, waiting to kiss his hand and receive his benediction. He,
submitting to it all with the utmost patience, was
fully ten minutes in getting down to his carriage,
assisted most obsequiously by noblemen and officers,
as eagerly soliciting his blessing as the poorest beg-
gars, and whose flashing orders, gold embroidered
uniforms, and uncovered heads, were in strange and
striking contrast to their usual haughty demeanor.

In the afternoon F—— and I took the steamer for
Peterhof to see the illumination in the park in honor

of the Czarina, — standing a mortal hour in the file, under a hot sun, waiting our turn to embark; the same thing having to be gone through with on the long wooden pier when we came back.

The full description of the illuminations, the crowd, the superb horses and liveries, the nobility, and all that we saw during the night (we reached St. Petersburg and our hotel at three A. M.), would be simply impossible : the fountains, the long drives through the woods of the park, the Summer Palace, parterres, and moat, the trees, — everything and everywhere for about five miles one vast blaze of colored lights. Imagine a new firmament, or read the Arabian Nights tales! The number of lights must have been in the millions. I counted four thousand on eight screens about one fountain, and this was to the illumination what one drop of water would be to a river. It was a marvelously beautiful sight, and in its way one of the most interesting we saw in Russia; showing so strikingly the power and control in an absolute monarchy of the emperor over his resources and subjects, when able to spend such a sum of money and such an inconceivable amount of labor on the mere pleasure and amusement of a single evening. One of the most striking features was a summer-house, with marble bust of the Czar and Czarina on either side, in the middle of a small lake, one blaze of light. It appeared like a huge fairy crown, created for the moment by a magician's wand: so airy, so light, so ethereal, that it seemed impossible to think of it as the work of human hands.

The Summer Palace — a long, low, rather rococo building, with pavilions at either end, surmounted with golden minarets and domes — is situated on an elevation, similar in location to *Sans Souci* at Potsdam. From the parterre in front of it a huge fountain staircase, adorned with gilded statuary (copies of antiques: Perseus, Meleager, Hercules, Discoboli; Venus of Milo, Medici, etc.), descends to the level of the park, with wide stairways for ascending and descending on either side. From its foot, a canal, or moat, crossed by numerous ornamental bridges, extends through thick woods, out to the gulf. Hundreds of fountains, throwing huge jets of water and spray in all directions, — running and falling in miniature water-falls over the numerous steps and amongst the golden statuary to the moat at

the bottom,—were illuminated by throwing different
colored lights on the moving, flowing mass: whilst
the façade of the palace, the steps, the statuary, the
parterre, the canal, the bridges, the trees on either
side, and away out on the gulf the ships and boats,
were all covered with millions of red and green and
blue and yellow, and every-colored lights; in great
groups of one color in places, in others mixed or
graduated, — apparently as countless and unnum-
bered as the stars in the heavens.

All this was but one small part of the general
illumination, which extended on this same scale for
several miles. It all seemed like one vast, beautiful
dream of fairyland.

The Czar and Czarina, followed by the whole Imperial household, drove about the grounds all the
evening. The Czarina's carriage was drawn by eight
dappled grey stallions, with postilions and outriders.
He sat silent and glum, most of the time smoking
a cigarette. She was queenly and beautiful, dressed
all in white, bowing gracefully, and sweetly smiling
to all. They passed us frequently during the evening. There was no guard, — not a soldier about or
near them. Any one in the vast throngs—and there

must have been hundreds of thousands, of all ages, sex, and conditions — could at any time during the evening have approached to the very carriage wheels : rather of a contradiction to the absurd newspaper reports one reads of the Emperor's secluded, guarded life, and his fears of Nihilistic attempts. The enthusiasm was intense. We could always judge of his whereabouts by the shouts and vivas that filled the air. A great wave of sound followed him wherever he drove.

The Summer Garden, opposite the vast bare July 23, Champs de Mars, is a large park, with dense shade- (Aug. 4.) trees, which form a cool, quiet retired spot in the heart of the city. Numerous rude, coarse marble statues ornament (?) the central walk at one end, near which are a fine railing, entrance gate, and commemorative chapel.

The Gostinnoë Dvor, a vast bazaar, occupies the entire space between four streets, opposite our hotel. I had read of this place from the time of my boyish days, and had always been curious to see it. It was different in every way from what I expected to see : simply a collection of shops for the sale of modern foreign wares, chiefly clothing and dress goods, with wholesale stores above. One walks under arcades about the entire structure and on both stories, outside on the street façades, and inside about a central square.

After dinner F—— and I took another drive around the islands. It is a pleasant, restful way of passing a few hours, in a comfortable carriage,—with thick rubber tires to break the noise, shock, and jar of the pavements,—behind a pair of black stallions, bowling along at a rate of ten or twelve miles an hour.

There is a curious custom at night in St. Petersburg of porters ('watch-dogs' we called them) on all doorsteps and entrances of hotels, palaces, and the better class of houses, where they lie curled up in their great fur coats. No matter how soundly they sleep, no one can approach or enter without their springing up and opening the door.

All servants, porters, help, and attachés always rise on one's approach, standing in a respectful and submissive attitude while one is walking by them.

Our permits have at last arrived from the Ministers for entrance to the Winter Palace; so that, if we can get our passport in time from the police, we shall leave to-morrow night for Moscow. A serious business this passport visé in Russia. They have one completely at their mercy, and it is fully as hard to get away as to enter the country. The river all the way up at night is patrolled by police boats, burning red lights, which must be signalled by passing craft of every description.

In regard to language, we find German and French universally spoken by people with any education,— especially the former. The only trouble is with the droski drivers, who speak only Russian. As there is no tariff of fares, and the alphabetical characters are such that no foreigner can make them out or write them, it is rather difficult to drive a bargain, or to indicate where one wishes to be taken.

Spent two hours in the Winter Palace to-day. A fairly comfortable building, noticeable chiefly for the vast number and extent of its rooms, corridors, and staircases, with pleasant views out over the river from various balconies. In the different halls and rooms we were shown a large collection of paintings of all the chief battles in which Russia has ever taken part ; also, portraits of all the emperors and celebrated Russian generals and men. One room

July 24, (Aug. 5.)

is finished and furnished entirely with malachite; mantelpiece, tables, standing candelabra, an immense ornamental vase, and all around the four walls large supporting columns of the same. In others the furniture was of the most ordinary description, with evidences of rococo and imitation lapis lazuli and marbles in many places. The Throne Room, rather gaudily decorated with gold, contained a picture said to be a Raphael, — 'The Resurrection.'

July 25,   Arrived early at the curious old Eastern town of
(Aug. 6.)

MOSCOW.

A wet, rainy day. The streets, which are badly paved, are filthy with mud and running water. This is the first day since leaving home that the weather has interfered with our sight-seeing. The drainage is very poor, the smells are sickening, the droskies are detestable. We sadly miss the broad, imperial thoroughfares and swiftly running vehicles of St. Petersburg. A greater contrast than between the two cities can scarcely be imagined. Moscow is unlike anything that we have ever seen. The architecture on all sides is most bizarre and interesting. The buildings and walls of the Kremlin, the towers and onion-shaped domes, of which there are hundreds to be seen in any direction one may look, are glaring with gold and flaming colors. The Moskowa River winds through the city past one side of the Kremlin wall, adding to the picturesqueness, the filthiness, and the odors of the place.

The people are devotional even to idolatry. In a small chapel, by one of the entrance gates to the Kremlin, is a curious figure of the Virgin, blackened with age; except the face, feet, and hands, it is covered with gold and adorned with precious stones. It is supposed to be endowed with extraordinary powers of healing and forgiveness. All day long the crowd of passers-by enter to prostrate themselves to the very ground in front of it, kissing devoutly and reverently the hands and feet of the figure. This is the famous Iberian Mother of God. It is enclosed in a case with handles, and is taken out daily and driven about before the kneeling multitudes, or upon payment of a large sum to the houses of the sick to cure them of their diseases. A special coach with four horses is devoted to its use, the attendants riding always with uncovered heads. At night, I have seen the square in front of it full of sleeping groups, waiting for the opening of the chapel doors in the morning.

The Holy Gate of the Kremlin, curiously and rudely decorated with Oriental frescoing, is also an object of great veneration. It is never passed through, not even by the Emperor, except with uncovered head. This is even exacted of strangers.

We spend the whole day in the cathedrals and Palace of the Kremlin. Every portion of the interiors of the cathedrals is profusely decorated with large figures of emperors, saints, apostles, and martyrs, on gold backgrounds. The Icon of the great cathedral is superb with its heavily ornamental gold columns and panels. Even the supporting pillars about the building do not escape this contagion of gold and color. The result is a *tout ensemble* of color and sparkle such as I have never seen in civilized countries. All this, with the curious shapes and profusion of external domes and minarets, keeps one constantly on the alert for the unexpected, and is a continual reminder of the remoteness and Eastern character of this most strange city. A raised dais in the centre of the great cathedral of the Kremlin is the spot where all the Emperors of Russia have been crowned.

The Kremlin Palace is worthy of all praise. It
consists of the ancient and modern residences of the
Emperors. The large modern Throne, Reception,
and Audience chambers, with superb effects in white
and gold, are three noble rooms; the largest I have
ever seen, with floors of polished marqueterie. The
Emperor's dais, chair, and baldaquin in the Throne
Room are truly regal, with covered steps of the finest
gold woven carpet. The Imperial eagles behind the
chair are massively wrought. The immense panels
of the walls are upholstered with embossed Persian
silk of a delicate blue, while the columns and ceiling
are of white stucco, covered with golden arabesques
and Persian characters. It is in this room that the
Emperors give audience immediately after their coronation. The Empress receives the congratulations
of the ladies in a smaller, adjacent room, in which
the dais, baldaquin, and chair are of scarlet silk
velvet. After coronation and audience, a dinner is
served in the dining-room of the older palace. This
room is most unique in shape and size. A huge
square column in the centre, around which is the
buffet, supports the sectionally arched monastic
ceilings, which, with the walls, are adorned with

Biblical subjects, on a gold background. Around the four sides, a low settee is covered with delicately embroidered Persian silks, which contrast with a most bizarre floor carpet, of curious Oriental designs, in dark material, on an orange foundation.

In the old Palace of the Czars the apartments are low, small, dimly lighted; almost weird and monastic. The walls and ceilings are decorated with a dark mixture of Eastern colors and characters. The floors and stairways of stone, carefully and curiously hewn into the same characters, make a very uneven and uncomfortable footing to walk upon. The effect of all this seemed curiously to impress one with an idea of absolute despotic rule and weird, uncanny power. One walked cautiously and hesitatingly, as if half expecting suddenly to come upon some fierce caliph who held one's life in his hands.

In the square outside of these buildings, at the foot of the tall Ivan Bell-tower, is the great Moscow bell, of bronze and silver, weighing over two hundred tons, nearly five times the height of an ordinary man, and sixty-seven feet in circumference. It is now raised on a low pedestal, with the broken piece by its side.

Around the Arsenal building are several curious and ornamental bronze guns and gun carriages. One huge piece at the corner, weighing forty tons, is a suitable companion for the great bell.

Our first general view of the city was from the Kremlin wall; but, owing to the rain, we did not long linger, anticipating an ascent of the Bell-tower the first pleasant day.

Most of the restaurants in Moscow are thoroughly Slav, in decoration, cooking, and attendance. One is served by natives dressed all in white, with a red sash at the waist. The wines are excellent, the soups are iced; fish follows the meat; their coffee and tea are unrivalled; and for a first course, fresh caviare on toast or warm bread is delicious when taken with a fiery native drink (somewhat resembling schnapps), as an appetiser.

Near the Holy Gate of the Kremlin is the Cathedral of St. Basile, with its eleven extraordinary domes, no two of which are alike. It is architecturally the most remarkable building in Russia. One can only liken it to a huge vegetable garden of brick and metal, painted in all the colors of the rainbow. Its interior seems to consist of a series of small chapels.

One of the most conspicuous buildings in Moscow is the modern Church of the Deliverer, built since 1814, to commemorate the retreat of Napoleon. It is in the shape of a Greek cross, of sandstone, with five golden domes, situated on an eminence, surrounded by tasteful gardens, which are protected by embankment walls; it is grand and imposing, but seems curiously out of place, with its modern architecture and decorations, in this old town. The interior is most sumptuous and pleasing. A dado of dark marble is surmounted with the same material in grey and white, above which are frescoes of scriptural subjects. In the centre and top of the central lofty dome is a colossal fresco of The Almighty, with outstretched hands, in benediction. In the ends and above the entrance doors of each of three arms of the cross are balconies, protected by railings composed of a series of single brass candlesticks, which are also continued on the same level entirely around the walls. When we first entered, at dusk, evening service was going on, and these candles were all lighted, together with those in numerous gilt and *cloisonné* candelabra on the floor. The effect of strong light and dark shadow in the fast

darkening twilight was grand. The entrances under
the balconies are protected by finely wrought trel-
lised, bronze, screen doors. Numerous paintings
adorn the walls in panels between the marbles.

In the fourth arm of the cross is the altar, covered by a pyramidal-shaped chapel of white polished
marble, with numerous panel paintings of saints and
figures, all surmounted with gold bronze eagles and
cross on the crescent (indicating the triumph of the
one over the other) ; the entrance to the altar being
screened by massive golden doors, *percées à jour.*
This chapel reaches quite up to the ceiling of the
church.

Russian priests, with their long flowing hair
and superb golden robes, were chanting the service,
assisted by two choirs of men and boys, — one on
either side of the altar, — who took up the responses
singly or in unison. The marble walls and polished
surfaces acting like vast sounding-boards, the deep,
sonorous tones of the priest and the chorus of the
choirs lingered and reverberated about the building,
until they finally died away in the vast vault of the
dome above. It was all most impressive, the effect
being heightened by the evident sincerity and de-

votion of the worshippers, who prostrated themselves, according to the Russian custom, flat on the pavement, at intervals. We lingered for more than an hour, spell-bound by the delicious music and the sacred character of the service; all the while the deep and musical tones of hundreds of bells outside were chiming and calling to prayer all over the city.

We are stopping at the Slaviansky Bazar (Hotel du Bazar Slave), which was originally built, as its name indicates, for a bazaar; but, failing of success, it was converted into a hotel. The present restaurant was the former salesroom. It is very large and lofty, with tastefully painted and ornamented beams, arches, and buttresses. The tables are placed in niches around the walls, intended as stalls for the sale of goods. In the centre is a large basin with fountain, about which are numerous palm and other growing trees and green foliage. The cooking is excellent, and the room is most attractive.

Sunday,   Attended mass this morning in the Great Cathe-
July 26,   dral of the Kremlin. The officiating priests, with
(Aug. 7.) their Greek crowns and robes, might have been so
many old patriarchs, representations of whom we
are so familiar with in Biblical prints.

After the service we climbed the Ivan tower to view the city, and a marvellous and unusual sight it was. We looked down upon a sea of light green roofs, relieved by hundreds on hundreds of golden and colored towers and minarets. It was from this point that Mme. de Staël made her famous and excellent description of Moscow in three words : ' *Voilà Rome Tartare !* '

Toward evening we went up the river for about three miles, on a miserable little steamer, to the foot of Sparrow Hill, which we climbed to get the celebrated view which Napoleon, with his invading army, first had of the city. Thiers, in his ' History of the Consulate and Empire,' thus describes it : —

Enfin, arrivée au sommet d'un coteau, l'armée découvrit tout-à-coup au dessous d'elle, et à une distance assez rapprochée, une ville immense, brillante de mille couleurs, surmontée d'une foule de dômes dorés resplendissants de lumière, mélange singulier de bois, de lacs, de chaumières, de palais, d'églises, de clochers, ville à la fois gothique et byzantine, réalisant tout ce que les contes orientaux racontent des merveilles de l'Asie. Tandis que des monastères flanqués de tours formaient la ceinture de cette grande cité, au centre s'élevait sur une éminence une forte citadelle, espèce de capitole où se voyaient à la fois les temples de la Divinité et les palais des empereurs, où au dessus des murailles crénelées surgissaient des dômes majestueux, portant l'emblème qui représente toute l'histoire de la Russie et toute son ambition, la croix sur le croissant renversée. Cette citadelle c'était le Kremlin, ancien séjour des Tzars.

A cet aspect magique, l'imagination, le sentiment de la gloire, s'exaltant à la fois, les soldats s'écrièrent tous ensemble : ' Moscou ! Moscou ! ' Ceux qui étaient restés au pied de la colline se hatèrent d'accourir ; pour un moment, tous les rangs furent confondus, et tout le monde voulut contempler la grande capitale où nous avait con- duits une marche si aventureuse. On ne · pouvait se rassasier de ce spectacle éblouissant et fait pour éveiller tant de sentiments divers. Napoléon survint à son tour, et, saisi de ce qu'il voyait, lui qui avait, comme les plus vieux soldats de l'armée, visité successivement le Caire, Memphis, le Jourdain, Milan, Vienne, Berlin, Madrid, il ne put se défendre d'une profonde émotion.

We strolled through the birch woods and over the hill, for an hour ; and after a delicious cup of tea, with a slice of lemon, from a smoking samovar which was brought to our table at a little restaurant by the river, we took steamer back to the city. The

Moskowa describes, in its course through and about Moscow, an immense letter S; thus we had many excellent views on our return. The rain had ceased, the clouds all disappeared, and the air had that peculiar clear, transparent effect which is so often noticeable after a storm. As we approached the city nearer and nearer, every golden spire stood out clearly and distinctly against the sky ; while the last rays of the setting sun glistened and gleamed from dome to dome. We landed on the island below the Kremlin, and, as we walked back on the opposite side of the river, the old citadel, with its walls, towers, and buildings, was magical to behold.

We saw the peasants all the afternoon, farming, fishing, and gathered on the banks of the stream to watch us pass. They seem a good-natured, ignorant, low class, much given to drunkenness, and astonishingly fond of the various shades of red. It is used both by male and female to such an extent in clothing as to be almost typical. The men dress with top boots, creased and folded at the ankle, dark trousers tucked into the boots, and a red shirt, either of flannel or cotton, worn like a blouse, with a belt or string at the waist ; over this, as the weather re-

quires, they put on a vest and coat, and on top of all,
a peculiar, flowing, long-tailed overcoat. The effect
of the vest only, worn over the shirt, with the red
flaps flying below it, is very curious. A black cloth
cap, with visor, completes the costume. Most of
the women have a dress, apron, waist, or at least a
handkerchief tied over the head, either of scarlet or
pink; often both colors are worn at the same time.
The waist of the dress is so short that in many cases
the skirt hangs from above the bosom. These red
shirts and dresses, everywhere dotted about, in the
fields and on the water, are very picturesque, and
give bits of warm color to the landscape.

July 27,   We spent the morning wandering through the
(Aug. 8.) intricacies of the Gostinnoë Dvor, which I found
much nearer my ideal than the St. Petersburg
bazaar. It covers many squares, through which the
narrow streets run, with passageways innumerable.
After the first turn or two, one loses all idea of
locality, and wanders about through a labyrinth of
turnings, midst a bewildering and confusing assort-
ment of tempting wares.

F—— left me at noon for Warsaw and Germany.
I then presented my letters of introduction, and

received for the next four days, both in Moscow and
at Nijni, a generous welcome and hospitality, which
will always remain one of the pleasantest recollections of my trip in Russia.

NIJNI NOVGOROD.

During the period of the fair at Nijni, smoking   July 28
in the streets is prohibited, under a penalty of 500   (Aug. 9.)
roubles (a rouble is nominally worth about seventy-
five cents). Notices to this effect are posted everywhere ; but, unfortunately for me, they were all in
Russian characters. As I drove from the station on
my arrival, enjoying a good cigar and the fresh
morning air, after a tiresome, sleepless night in a
close railway carriage, a mounted official stopped my
droski before we had gone the length of two blocks.
Evidently something was seriously wrong ; but what
it was I could not ascertain. Even the production
of my passport failed to satisfy him. The address
on my letter of introduction to the resident English
Consul produced more effect, and calling a second
guard, who seated himself by my side, we drove on.
With this escort of foot and horse, I presented myself — or rather was presented, for I was under

arrest — at the residence of the Consul. Mutual explanations followed, and the affair (which might have been most serious for me) was amicably arranged. This was but one of the many obligations, and but the beginning of the courteous hospitality, I received from Mr. F—— during the day. With the joking remark that I evidently was not able to take care of myself alone, he remained with me during all the hours I spent at Nijni, thoughtfully providing for my fullest enjoyment and best appreciation of the many curious sights and scenes of the great fair.

The town is pleasantly situated at the junction of two rivers : one of which, the great Volga, rolls majestically on its course through the town and down the vast valley. One bank rises to quite a height, on which residences are built to the very top.

The Fair grounds are on a peninsula between the rivers and a canal, and are only used in the weeks between July 15th and August 25th. The long lines of buildings, shops, warehouses, large hotels, restaurants, etc., are closed during the remainder of the year, and in spring are under water. This shows the importance of the fair, when a whole section of a city can be abandoned for ten months of every year for the profits in trading during the other two. It is not a mere holiday exhibition fair (in the sense we mean when using the word), but a vast national entrepôt where the entire trading and exchange of commodities for the whole year are condensed into a few weeks. Tartars, Persians, Armenians, Chinese,— all the different tribes of inhabitants and neighbors from the various parts of the vast Empire,— bring their products in huge quantities, which they dispose of at wholesale, and then buy the manufactured articles of the more civilized provinces to take back with them. The gathering of people, the piles of merchandise, the bargaining, customs, manners, dress, amusements, activity, and life of this vast human beehive is wonderful to behold. Every quarter has its restaurant, with choir of young women in various costumes according to its nationality, — the imported Hungarian, with red jacket, gold braid and coy little top-boots with tassels ; the costume de ballet ; the Tartars, with scarcely any costume at all, — who sing at intervals on a small raised platform, and then go about with their little silver plates for collections.

I left at nine P. M. by train. The distance between Nijni and Moscow is 450 versts (a verst is about three-quarters of an English mile), and takes twelve hours and a half. The same distance between Manchester and London is done in five hours. From St. Petersburg to Moscow, 650 versts, takes about thirteen hours, which is the fastest train in Russia. The cars are very comfortable, some of them somewhat similar in general arrangement to the Pullman day car. The chairs extend, and can be pulled out at night to form a couch. This does very well, provided one travels, as the natives always do, with pillow and bed clothing. The stranger (except in the sleepers on the St. Petersburg train, which surpass even the Pullman) who goes without these may make up his mind to be cold and uncomfortable.

MOSCOW.

July 29, (Aug. 10.) I have escaped all three of the annoyances which are usually experienced during a trip to the Nijni Fair, — heat, dust, and bugs. Since the rain of Saturday and Sunday morning, the weather has been cool and delightful. Indeed, our whole Russian experience has been most enjoyable in every way.

The stories one hears of the surveillance and difficulties of travelling in the Empire are about as absurd as some of the ideas stay-at-home Englishmen have of America. Once have one's passport carefully prepared, give it up willingly to the police on arrival, never leave without it, behave prudently and conform to the laws, and there will be no interference, no surveillance, no restraint. One will find it as pleasant a country to travel in as any in Europe.

In a conversation with an Englishman at Scarborough, he impressed upon me the necessity of engaging a courier immediately on landing at St. Petersburg, going into an elaborate and confidential explanation of their relation to the government, during which he informed me that they were in reality regularly authorized detectives ; that in any event a watch would be set on my movements in some form or another, and that it would be much pleasanter to have it openly, in the shape of an assistant and interpreter, than to feel constantly that in some unseen and unknown way one's every step was dogged and followed. I now honestly believe that Englishman to be thoroughly mistaken in his ideas of the Russian police-system. We have travelled 1,600 miles in the country, have never for a single hour engaged the services of a courier, never for a moment been conscious of, or seen the most trifling indication of surveillance or espionage,— not even during the night of the Peterhof illuminations, where, as I have already stated, we were constantly in the presence of the Emperor and Empress for hours, and could have at any moment, and did several times, approach to the very wheels of their carriage. I have often seen the streets guarded by a cordon of police much more carefully for the passage of our presidents, than were the drives of Peterhof Park that evening.

More than all this, I believe there is an opportunity to make money in Russia by intelligent foreigners, owing to the absence of a middle-class. The nobles are too wealthy or haughty, and the moujik is yet too ignorant to work at a trade. The presence of so many Germans would seem to indicate this. We were informed that out of a population in St. Petersburg of nearly a million, there are over 200,000 of them. They are a prudent, thrifty people, and well know where their best interests lie. We also met many resident Scotchmen — engineers, contractors, and manufacturers — all busily engaged in pushing forward the various new lines of railway, and the great pipe conduits for oil, which are now receiving so much attention from the government and from capitalists in the Southern provinces.

The vast stretches of country between the large cities remind one of some of our Western tracts, and are capable, with intelligent cultivation, of great improvement.

Called on Dr. H——, whom I met in Sweden. He received me most cordially, and prevailed upon me to stay another day in Moscow. We drove out to Petrovski Park, stopping at the trotting grounds and training stables on our way. The palace is interesting on account of its curious architecture and the simplicity of its interior and furnishing. It is refreshing to be able to enter a building without being obliged to wonder and marvel at fresh treasures at every turn.

We dined well at a restaurant in the park, which also had its music, its Hungarian singers *en costume,* and a band of dark, willowy gypsies. *Toujours la femme en Russie!*

July 30,   Spent the whole of this my last day in Moscow
(Aug. 11.) lazily lounging through the Kremlin and about
the city, vividly photographing the now well-known
buildings and costumes on my mind forever more.
Left by train in the evening for

ST. PETERSBURG,

July 31,   where I arrived the next morning.   Spent the day
(Aug. 12.) in a droski, making sundry purchases, and arranging
to leave Russia on the morrow.

Aug. 1,   Spent the morning with Colonel Way, our Consul
(Aug. 13.) General.   At five P. M. sailed on the Wilson steamer
Marsdin, and began boxing the compass on our tort-
uous voyage back to England by sea.   I have now
done with the Julian calendar, and can again return
to single dates.   St. Petersburg is fading away in
the distance, as so many cities have done before on
this trip.   The sun lingers lovingly on St. Isaac's
and the golden Admiralty spire.   Good-bye, Russia,
good-bye!   I leave you, with your golden domes,
broad thoroughfares, and strange people, very unwillingly.   You have taken a strong hold on me.   Shall
I ever see you again!